Gary Jones

South Africa

This book was professionally typeset on Reedsy.
Find out more at reedsy.com

Contents

1

Introduction

Over the years, South Africa has gained the curiosity of many, and is now considered as one of the best tourist destinations on earth. Now that it's an open democratic country, and with a vast cultural diversity, it's definitely a hotspot of adventures and filled with travel spots that you never thought possible!

South Africa has some of the best beaches in the world, and you will be able to experience them from the West Coast all the way to the

Indian Ocean along the vast coastline of South Africa.

Wildlife is, of course, also big in South Africa. In places such as the Eastern Cape or Kruger National Park, among others, you'd be able to see elephants, jackals, lions, hippos, elephants, buffalos, and many other animals in their natural habitat!

Aside from that, you'd also be able to be one with nature, spend some time under the sun, and frolic in the sea or traverse the mountains! South Africa gives plenty of hiking and paragliding opportunities, together with the chance to go around the provinces by bike, and you can explore forest canopies, too!

When you're tired, you could chill out and relax by cooling down in Cape Winelands, or enjoy gourmet meals in Kwa-Zulu Natal Midlands. Even while eating, you'll still be able to bask in the majestic beauty of South Africa!

History also abounds. Africa is home to Robben Island, where former President Nelson Mandela was once held by the Apartheid government and is also home to one of the oldest fossils in the world—as old as 2.3

million years!

Aside from the fact that South African people are very friendly, you can also be sure that you'll get value for your money. Entrance fees to various museums or parks are quite affordable, and you don't have to stay in luxury hotels—you can choose family-run lodges or guesthouses, and enjoy meals at nearby vintage restaurants, too.

In short, there's certainly a lot to see, and a lot to do—and you'll definitely be able to bask in the glory that South Africa brings.

South Africa has 9 provinces or states.In this guide, we will explore South Africa together by looking at all the provinces in separate chapters.All the other important information like how to get around the country, the weather and safety all gets covered in different chapters.I think you will find this book very practical because we included the best of South Africa with links to online maps and other resources to make your trip as convenient as possible.

Read this guide now, and start planning your trip!

Thank you and enjoy!

2

Getting Into and Getting Around South Africa

So, first things first. Of course, you have to know how to get into South Africa and get around town before being able to do anything. Mostly, you can get into South Africa by using its three main international airports, namely:

Three Main SA Airports
Johannesburg International Airport (JIA)

Seated at the foot of Kempton Park in Gauteng, South Africa, Johannesburg Airport has certainly evolved from how it was when it was established in 1952. Now, the airport is totally neat and has been constructed to house the Airbus A380, and is very easy to reach because the Gautrain Rapid Rail Link is just situated above it.

Gautrain Rapid Rail Link Website

http://www.gautrain.co.za/

Usually, there are flights to JIA from: Washington, New York (JFK), Jeddah, Cairo, Tel Aviv, Sao Paulo (Guarulhos), Buenos Aires, Sydney, Perth, Melbourne, Hong Kong, Kuala Lumpur, Singapore, Abu Dhabi, Doha, Dubai, Frankfurt, Munich, Amsterdam, London (Heathrow), Lisbon, Madrid

To contact JIA, just call: +27(0)11921-6911

Johannesburg International Airport (JIA) Website

http://www.airports.co.za/airports/or-tambo-international

Johannesburg International Airport (JIA) Map

https://goo.gl/maps/JWJaqVZoHrq

Cape Town International Airport (CPT).

This is the primary airport in Cape Town, South Africa and is known as the third busiest in all of Africa. Back in 1954, it was the only airport in South Africa that provided scheduled flights in Africa, was renovated for the 2010 World Cup—and has since gotten the respect of many travelers all over the world!

It serves flights for most of the cities that JIA serves, and also seasonal flights to and from: Zurich, Paris, Frankfurt, Munich.

You can contact the airport at: +27 21 937 1275

You can hail a taxi in front of the airport terminal, or ride the MyCiti Bus.

Cape Town International Airport (CPT) Website

http://www.airports.co.za/airports/cape-town-international

Cape Town International Airport (CPT) Map

https://goo.gl/maps/8RzuMrHsTdT2

More city transport information is found here:

City Transport Website

http://myciti.org.za/en/home/

Durban King Shaka International Airport

Durban is also known as King Shaka International Airport. The thing is it does not serve a lot of international flights, so you may have to get connecting flights. However, what's good is that it's near most hotels and beaches, which most travelers find to be extremely helpful. You can also book for your flight without paying anything!

You can contact the airport at: 032 436 6758

King Shaka International Airport Website

http://www.airports.co.za/airports/king-shaka

King Shaka International Airport Map

https://goo.gl/maps/6979M1LXRkF2

Domestic Airlines

Now, if you're going to get around the country, you could also make use of South Africa's Domestic Airlines. The best ones are:

Mango Airlines

This is deemed as a no-frills carrier under that offers single-class, low-cost flights between Cape Town, Durban, Johannesburg, Bloemfontein, and Port Elizabeth.

For reservations, you may call: +27 11 978 1111 or call the help desk at: 0861 1 MANGO (0861 162 646)

Mango Air Website

https://www.flymango.com/

Kulula Airlines

This offers low-cost single class flights between Port Elizabeth, George, Durban, Cape Town, Johannesburg, and Nelspruit. It also offers flights from Tambo International Airport in Johannesburg to Durban, George, Port Elizabeth, and Cape Town.

You may call the help desk at: 0861 KULULA (585 852)

For international bookings, you may reach them at: +27 11 921 0111

You may also email them at: info@kulula.com
Kulula Airlines Website
http://www.kulula.com/

Airlink and SA Express

This airline flies locally between Mthatha, Johannesburg, Durban, Cape Town, Margate, Hoedspruit, Kimberley, Mmbatho, Manzini, Mozro, Richards Bay, and Upington, as well as to Madagascar, Zimbabwe, and Zambia. You may choose from first class, business, or economy.

You may call the help desk at: +27 11 961 1700

For international bookings, you may call: +27 11 978 5313

You may also email them at: info@flyairlink.com

Airlink Website

http://www.flysaa.com/za/en/footerlinks/aboutUs/Airlink.html

SA Express Website

http://www.flyexpress.aero/

South African Airways

This is a national carrier that flies between Cape Town, Johannesburg, East London, Port Elizabeth, Durban, Richards Bay, George, Masero, Manzini, and Upington. It can also connect to flights around Africa and the rest of the world!

For reservations, call: +27 11 978 1111

For international bookings, call: +27 11 978 5313

You may also email them at: help@flysaa.com

South African Airways Website

http://www.flysaa.com/gb/en/home.action

British Airways

And finally, you also have British Airways that provides return flights from the Kruger National Park, Port Elizabeth, Durban, and Cape Town. You may also choose from first class, club/business, premier economy, or economy.

For reservations, call: +27 11 441 8400

British Airways Website

http://www.britishairways.com/travel/home/public/en_za

Public Transport

Of course, you also need to know how you'd be able to get around town by land. You actually have a lot of choices, and you can find out more about them below!

By Bus

Baz Bus

One of travelers' favorite bus companies is Baz Bus, which is known as a door to door, hop on-hop off service that can pick you up from around 160 hostels in 40 different South African towns! It's definitely a convenient way to roam around, as you'd feel like you wouldn't have to go and hail a bus on your own!

The buses are all 22-seaters, and you'd have a chance to watch your favorite movies or television shows, too! You can also ask the driver or ask for an info sheet regarding where you should go, and what you should avoid! It's like having your own tour guide! You can ride the bus without any time limit as long as you're going in one direction between:

Cape Town Johannesburg / Johannesburg Cape Town

Cape Town Durban / Durban Cape Town

Cape Town Port Elizabeth / Port Elizabeth Cape Town

For questions or reservations, you may call: +27 21 422 5202.

You may also email them at: info@bazbus.com

Baz Bus Website

http://www.bazbus.com/

Baz Bus Map

https://goo.gl/maps/6QSUF6AayUy

Intercape

Meanwhile, Intercape offers charter buses with Sleepliner seats that are really comfortable because they allow passengers to recline up to 180 degrees and can go around Cape Town, Beaufort West, Kimberley, George, East London, and Durban.

For queries or reservations, you may call: +27 21 380 4400

You may also email them at: info@intercape.co.za

Intercape Website

http://www.intercape.co.za/

Greyhound

This company offers some of the most popular public buses around. In fact, Greyhound buses have the distinction for being the people's choice in going around South Africa. They have various routes in the provinces of Kwa-Zulu Natal, Western Cape, Eastern Cape, Limpopo, Free State, and Gauteng. They also provide services to and from Zimbabwe and Mozambique.

For questions and reservations, you may call them at: 011 611 8000 or 083 915 9000

Greyhound Website
https://www.greyhound.co.za/
You may also try the following bus companies:
Translux (0861 589 282)
Eldo Coaches (011 213 9953)
City to City (0861 589 282)
It's also recommended that you book bus tickets at Computicket.
Computicket Website
http://online.computicket.com/web/

By Train

You can also travel around town by train. Here are some of those train companies that you should set your sights on:

The Blue Train

This is considered as one of the world's most luxurious and reliable railways. Not only will you get to your destination in time, you'll also be able to enjoy perfect and picturesque scenery between Cape Town and Pretoria. One whole route would be around 27 hours, but you can expect to be treated to posh seating and sleeping arrangements, together with gourmet cuisine!

For reservations, you may call +27 12 334 8459

For questions and for more information, you may email: info@blue-train.co.za

The Blue Train Website
http://www.bluetrain.co.za/

The Shosholoza Meyl Premier Classe

This is known as an upmarket train service that travels between Cape Town and Johannesburg, and Durban and Johannesburg each week. You can choose between single or double coupes or family compartments. Meals and bedding are also included in the fare!

For more information, contact: 011 773 9247

The Shosholoza Meyl Premier Classe Website
http://southafricanrailways.co.za/premier_classe.html

Urban Commuter Trains

You may also try Urban Commuter Trains, or those trains that move fast in metropolitan areas. You can try:

Gautrain

This basically links Gauteng, Pretoria, and Johannesburg together to provide efficient and comfortable travels for commuters. It also provides alternative routes for tourists who are longing for quick day trips between the said cities.

For more information, contact: 0800 428 87246

Gautrain Website

http://www.gautrain.co.za/

Vintage Train Travel

And, if you're looking to go the classic route, you may also try vintage trains, which are around due to the hard work of independent operators. It's a good way of giving back to the locals and seeing South Africa, too!

You may try:

Friends of the Rail

This one is operated by enthusiasts who are committed to the preservation of South Africa's coach and steam train heritage, running each day from Pretoria to the historic diamond village of Culinan. If going as a group with 15 people in, you get at least 10% discount, and you can even get a one way ticket with 70% off the regular price!

For more information, you may call 012 767 7913.

You may also email them at: sales@friendsoftherail.com

Friends of the Rail Website

http://www.friendsoftherail.com/joomla/

Umgeni Steam Railway

Meanwhile, this one is a 100-year old system engine located just near Durban. It services passengers moving along the Valley of the Thousand Hills, usually during each month's last Sunday.

Umgeni Steam Railway Website

http://www.umgenisteamrailway.co.za/BookingForm3_MyGate2015_2016.php

Atlantic Rail

This runs from Cape to Simon Town via the Cape Peninsula, providing excellent views for passengers who would like to see. Passengers would also be able to ride vintage coaches dating back to 1922 to 1938, which will make the ride a whole lot more spectacular!

Atlantic Rail Website

http://www.atlanticrail.co.za/

Taxis

In the major cities taxis are available in the major cities,howeer makes sure its a registere taxi to make sure you stay safe.In the major cities like Cape Town and Johannesburg Uber is available.

Uber Cape Town Website

https://www.uber.com/cities/cape-town/

Uber Johannesburg Website

https://www.uber.com/cities/johannesburg/

3

Weather of the 9 Provinces

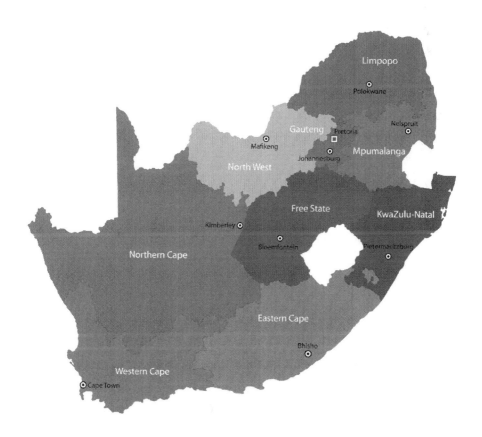

Of course, if you're going to travel around South Africa, you do have to check the state of the weather in order to protect yourself from harsh weather conditions, and make sure your trip would be hassle-free!

In this chapter, you'd learn more about the weather of the 9 South African Provinces!

Eastern Cape

Climate in the Eastern Cape is quite complicated and varied. The Eastern Cape experiences really hot summers (January to July) where temperature ranges between 16 to 36C, and cold winters (April to August), the temperature falls to 7 to 10C. Snowfalls are common during this season, especially in Rhodes and Molteno, two mountainous regions in South Africa.

As for the other months, they are mostly dry with sparse rain, especially in Port Elizabeth.

The Free State

A continental climate is prevalent in the Free State. This means they have hot summers and cool to cold winters, with frequent snow falls in the higher ranges of the province. It's a different story in the West, though, because summers are extremely hot there.

During the summer, there are brief thunderstorms because of precipitation, and some aridity in the west. Fittsburg, Bethlehem, and Harrismith are all well-watered, while there are hot, moist summers in Bloemfontein.

Summer is between January to July, with temperatures averaging 16 to 38C.

Gauteng

Next in the list is Gauteng, where the climate is mostly influenced by altitude. This is because some of the towns in the said province, such as Pretoria and Johannesburg are at 4,344 ft and 5,577 ft above sea level, respectively.

Brief thunderstorms during afternoons are signs of precipitation, and even if it becomes humid at times, it's still quite comfortable. In Southern areas, winters could be crisp and frosty, but snow is rare in metropolitan areas, such as Johannesburg.

From January to June, temperatures average 16 to 33 C; other times, it's colder.

Kwazulu-Natal

Another province with varied climate, Kwazulu-Natal also has complex topography, which is mostly verdant, but with coastlines and seas nearby. Mostly, Kwazulu-Natal has subtropical climate. However, you can expect that it's colder in inland regions.

An average of 21 to 28 C is prevalent during the months of January to March in Durban. During these times, rainfall may reach up to 1000mm. By June to August, temperature could be between 11 to 23 C, which could be even colder in the hinterlands, especially in Pietermaritzburg that experiences extremely cold winters.

In the summer (January to March), Tugela River Valley's Ladysmith could experience temperatures up to 30 C, but could also drop below freezing level in the evenings. Meanwhile, Zululand North Coast experiences the highest amount of humidity and the warmest climate out of anything else.

Snow is experienced in the Drakensberg, especially in its highest peaks.

Limpopo

Limpopo has one of the hottest climates in all of South Africa. This is because it is mostly situated near the Tropic of Capricorn in the equator, but if you want to travel during dry, sunny days, you definitely can experience it here.

The months of October to March are considered summer months, where temperature can average up to 30 C. Summer months may also bring forth some thunderstorms, even when the weather is extremely hot, especially in the eastern regions of the province. Temperatures in the peak of summer could reach 40C or higher.

Polokwane, Limpopo's capital city often has the best weather in the province, with just the right amount of sunshine regardless of the season. However, you have to expect that temperature really drops at night so you have to make sure that you get to keep yourself warm in the winter months.

Mpumalanga

Apart from a unique name, Mpumalanga, especially Lowveld, also boasts of subtropical climate—making it a perfect destination for many. This is because it is in proximity to the latitude and the Indian Ocean. The Lowfeld is also frost-free.

Higher spots, such as Highveld, experiences cool weather mostly because it's around 2300 to 1700 ft above sea level.

Thunderstorms are frequent in the Drakensberg Escarpment as it also experiences the most precipitation. This also means that the place is well-watered because of the said thunderstorms. Rain during the winter season is scarce.

Between the months of January to July, temperatures could range between 19 to 29 C, and around 6 to 23 C for the other months.

The Northern Cape

Next up is the Northern Cape. This province mostly experiences around 400 mm or 8 to 16 inches of rainfall each year, making it an arid to semi-arid area. However, rainfall increases from east to west, with around 20 to 540mm each year, where rain comes mostly from summer thunderstorms.

The Northern Cape also experiences some of the hottest temperatures along the Namibian Border in South Africa, with summer temperatures averaging to 30 to 45 C.

Southern areas are often bitterly cold, with clear and frosty winters. Snow is also experienced in these areas, especially in Sutherland.

From January to June, temperatures may average 18 to 35 C in Kimberley; 15 to 38 C in Springbok, and 9 to 27 C in Sutherland.

North West

Because of its proximity to the Kalahari Desert, North West has year-round sunshine, especially in its capital city of Mafikeng. However, even when sunshine is around, some towns still experience cool weather.

August to March are considered as the summer months, where temperatures average between 24 to 36 C, with around 300 to 700 mm of rainfall in a year. Summer means that days are sunny and dry, while nights could be chilly.

Meanwhile, winter season provides around 2 to 20 C of temperature, with some thunderstorms in the afternoon.

Western Cape

Finally, there's the Western Cape. You can expect a climatologically diverse weather in this province because of its varied topography, with micro and macro climates brought upon by the currents of nearby oceans.

These currents are the Benguela Current from the South Atlantic Ocean, and Agulhas Current going towards the East Coast, which makes the weather reminiscent of Mediterranean Islands, with dry summers, and cool and wet winters.

Meanwhile, arid to semi-arid climate is experienced in Little and Great Karoo, where thunderstorms are prevalent even during the summer months. Maritime weather is prevalent in the South Coast, especially in Overberg and Garden Route.

During the months of January to June, temperatures average 16 to 30 C, or 15 to 25 C in some provinces.Cape Town and surrounding areas can have extreme temperatures reaching a maximum of approximately 40 - 47 degrees Celsius during the peak of summer during December to February.

Weather Warning

South Africa has a wide variety of weather patterns.To be safe prepare for extremely hot weather and also sudden drops in temperature.In summer months, a hat and sunscreen will be very helpful.Although the winter could be mild compared to other countries, you should prepare for cold weather if you visit in the winter.South Africa is known for sudden extreme weather patterns.In today's context of climate change, it's even more important to prepare accordingly.

4

Tourist Visas in SA, Health, and Safety

VISA regulations in South Africa has become more lenient in the past few months as a means to improve tourism in the country, especially for residents of Russia, China, and India, who want to travel with their children and weren't able to do so before.

Basically, these days, all you have to do is make sure that your passport is valid for at least 6 months and beyond to be able to go to South Africa. Meanwhile, if you're from the Japan, Scandinavia, and most Commonwealth and European countries, you'd no longer have to apply for a VISA. You could get an automatic entry permit, which could last for a maximum of 30 days, and which you could get renewed while in South Africa! US Citizens can enter without a visa for up to 90 days.

Visa Requirements Website

http://www.home-affairs.gov.za/index.php/countries-exempt-from-sa-visas

Health and Safety

Before traveling to South Africa, it's also important to talk about health and safety precautions. This way, you'll know what you can expect, and you would be able to protect yourself and know where to ask for help in case of emergencies.

Medical Care and Safety Equipment

It's safe to say that South Africa now has some of the world's best medical facilities and infrastructure, with high standards of water treatment and doctors who are sought all over the world.

There are public and private hospitals all around South Africa, but if you're going to choose private hospitals, you have to make sure that your health insurance is adequate to cover what those hospitals might charge you with.Private Medical care is expensive in South Africa so make sure to get travel insurance.One of the top healthcare providers in all major cities is Mediclinic.

Mediclinic South Africa Website

http://www.mediclinic.co.za/Pages/default.aspx

Health Concerns

Malaria is considered by many as one of the major health concerns in South Africa. However, you have to remember that this is only a bit prevalent in Kwazulu-Natal's Maputaland Coast, as well as in Limpopo, Mpumalanga, and Lowveld. There is not much risk for this during the winter months, but you do have to be extra careful during hot summer months.

Malaria Map Website

http://www.fitfortravel.nhs.uk/destinations/africa/south-africa/south-africa-malaria-map.aspx

The South African Government has already been conducting an extensive anti-mosquito and anti-malaria program, with the help of Mozambique and Swaziland. In recent years, studies have proven that malaria incidences have been decreasing in number, and with the help of insect repellants, it's already easier to divert mosquitoes' attention away.

To protect yourself from Malaria while in South Africa, you could apply some insect repellent lotion or oil, wearing long sleeves and trousers, and making use of mosquito nets.

You can also take Malaria Prophylaxis, or medicine that's supposed to protect you from infected mosquitoes; you have to make sure that you take them a week or two before entering a malaria-prone area, and that you should follow package directions and not self-medicate. You should also continue taking the drugs for at least 2 to 4 weeks after leaving the malaria-prone area. Make sure to ask your medical practitioner about malaria medication and other vaccinations before your departure.

Food and Water

Top-notch food preparation is implemented in all major cities and towns in South Africa. You can also be sure that tap water is free of harmful micro-organisms, but if you want to really stay safe and be preventive, you could bring your own bottled water, too. Fresh fruits are also safe to eat.

Personal Safety Tips

Finally, before going to South Africa, it would also be essential to keep these personal safety tips in mind:

- If you have doubts about safety in certain areas, make sure to get the number of the nearest police station and get advice.
- Know emergency numbers by heart! For South Africa, you have:

10111 (National Emergency Response Hotline)
112 (Cell Phone Emergency Hotline)
10177 (Ambulance Hotline)

- Keep yourself from walking in unknown areas alone at night. If you really want to go out at night, go somewhere you're familiar with and make sure to bring someone with you.
- Don't make others feel like you don't know what you're doing or you have no idea where you are, because would just make you gullible and vulnerable.
- Always pre-set emergency numbers on your phone, especially before going to bed so in case something wrong happens, you could easily ask for help.
- Avoid carrying large amounts of money and wearing lots of jewelry while out in the open.
- Choose inns or spaces with security lights, or install some in your car.
- Do not use laundry facilities on your own at night.

- Carry purses or bags close to you—not with dangling straps.
- Don't mention that you'd be out of your room for a long time.And, avoid wearing anything that could restrict movement.

5

The 9 South African Provinces and their Languages

Next, it's also important to learn more about the 9 South African Provinces and their languages.

For starters, **English and Dutch** used to be the main languages of South Africa, but in 1961, Dutch was dropped and was replaced by **Afrikaans**, which also have some Dutch influence in it. Aside from that, South Africa also has other languages, which are as follows:

- **Ndebele**
- **Sotho**
- **Northern Sotho**
- **Tswana**
- **Tonga**
- **Zulu**
- **Xhosa**
- **Venda**

According to the constitution, the official languages of the Republic are: **English, Afrikaans, SisWati, Sesotho, Sepedi, Setswana, Xitsonga, Ndebele, Zulu, and Xhosa.** This just goes to show that while English is mostly used, people in South Africa also have their own dialects based on where they live—which makes them bi or multilingual!

English is used by most people in South Africa, so you should be able to get around South Africa easily using only English.

Western Cape

The Western Cape has a one-of-a-kind language policy which aims to make use of three provincial languages in an equal manner. These are:

-English

-Xhosa

-Afrikaans

Aside from that, South African Sign Language is also used!

Eastern Cape

Next up is the Eastern Cape. Here, around 78% of people speak Xhosa while 10% speak Afrikaans, and the rest could understand English. This means that it may be helpful if you could try to learn Xhosa or Afrikaans a bit, even just the basic phrases, so it would be easy for you to go around and seek help from the locales!

Northern Cape

In the Northern Cape, most of the population speaks Afrikaans over any other language. Apart from Afrikaans, other languages used in Northern Cape are Tswana, Xhosa, and English. Some indigenous languages, such as Khwe and Nama are also used.

Free State

Meanwhile, in the Free State, there is a good variation of languages. Only 2% of people speak English fluently—although some members of the population also understand the language, but just can't speak it properly. 64% of the population speak Sotho, 12.7% speak Afrikaans, 7.5% speak Xhosa, 5.2% speak Tswana, and 4.4% speak Zulu.

Kwazulu-Natal

In Kwazulu-Natal, around 77.8% of people speak Zulu, the language that's unique to this province. Next to that is 13.2% people who speak English, followed by 3.4% people who speak Xhosa, and 1.6% people who speak Afrikaans.

Gauteng

In Gauteng, around 17.8% of people speak Zulu, and around 14.3%

speak English. 13.8% speak Afrikaans, while 11.6% speak Sotho, and 10.6% speak Northern Sotho—making it one of the most diverse provinces in terms of languages.

Limpopo

In Limpopo, you have to at least know any of their languages because people there mostly do not speak English—apart from some important and popular destinations, of course.

52.9% of people in Limpopo speak Northern Sotho, 17% speak Tonga, 16.7% speak Venda, and 2.6% speak Afrikaans.

North West

North West is another province where English isn't really prevalent except for some places, so you do have to learn at least some of their languages a bit.

63.4% of people speak Tswana, 9.0% speak Afrikaans, 5.8% speak Sotho, 5.5% speak Xhosa, and 3.7% speak Tsonga.

Mpumalanga

Finally, you have Mpumalanga where English is only spoken in some popular places. Otherwise, you could expect 27.7% of locales to speak Swati, 24.1% to speak Zulu, 10.4% to speak Tsonga, 10.1% to speak Ndebele, and 9.3% to speak Northern Sotho!

6

The Best of the Western Cape

Western Cape

Situated in the Southwestern part of South Africa, the Western Cape is the 4th largest province with around 5.8 million inhabitants, and was established in 1994 after the dissolution of the Cape Province.

Western Cape Map

https://goo.gl/maps/fBCoDdpB1C22

Cape Town

Its capital is Cape Town, which is the third most populous urban area in South Africa and has a seat in the National Parliament.Cape Town is a magnificent city with world class beaches, restaurants, bars, hotels, museums, art galleries, national parks and everything else a traveler is looking for.In 2014, Cape Town was rated as the top world city to visit by the New York Times.

Museums, Art Galleries and Historical Areas

Cape Town is an international city and has a mix of European and African culture.I have put together a list of the best museums and galleries for you to visit.

Bo-Kaap and De Waterkant Website

http://www.dewaterkant.com/dewaterkant-history.html

Bo-Kaap and De Waterkant Map

https://goo.gl/maps/JwLmL2MLvby

Church Square and the Slave Lodge Website

http://www.iziko.org.za/museums/slave-lodge

Church Square and the Slave Lodge Map

https://goo.gl/maps/1nAP85uw5DN2

Castle Military Museum Website

https://www.facebook.com/pages/Castle-of-Good-Hope/108751525824452

Castle Military Museum Map

https://goo.gl/maps/jUo48Nx8ZNA2

City Hall and Grand Parade Map

https://goo.gl/maps/Ca7aJEig1K42

Company's Garden Website

https://www.facebook.com/thecompanysgardenrestaurant/

Company's Garden Map

https://goo.gl/maps/VSmwq3Yowpp

Peers' Cave (Fish Hoek) Website

http://www.capepointchronicle.co.za/guides/walks-of-the-south/peers-cave-from-the-fish-hoek-side/

Peers' Cave Map

https://goo.gl/maps/pXJgHyFDqNR2

District Six Museum Website

http://www.districtsix.co.za/

District Six Museum Map

https://goo.gl/maps/bzyZ2B8iHmT2

Iziko Planetarium Website

http://www.iziko.org.za/museums/planetarium

Iziko Planetarium Map

https://goo.gl/maps/6PMXnbYu1h32

Irma Stern Museum Website

http://www.irmastern.co.za/

Irma Stern Museum Map

https://goo.gl/maps/k9KKWebmQLD2

Iziko South African Museum Website

http://www.iziko.org.za/museums/south-african-museum

Iziko South African Museum Map

https://goo.gl/maps/sCoszZoKa6J2

Heritage Museum Website

http://www.simonstown.com/museum/sthm.htm

Heritage Museum Map
https://goo.gl/maps/kHVa1yBXH9N2
Heart of Cape Town Museum Website
http://www.heartofcapetown.co.za/
Heart of Cape Town Museum Map
https://goo.gl/maps/vNW4Y62YbAn
South African Jewish Museum Website
http://sajewishmuseum.org.za/
South African Jewish Museum Map
https://goo.gl/maps/ruLPYtnrXg82
Robben Island Website
http://www.robben-island.org.za/
Robben Island Map
https://goo.gl/maps/5Xz7UbkbC592
St George's Cathedral Website
http://sgcathedral.co.za/
St George's Cathedral Map
https://goo.gl/maps/dmYsHBTJ8ut

South African National Gallery Website
http://www.iziko.org.za/museums/south-african-national-gallery
South African National Gallery Map
https://goo.gl/maps/Y2aJcaLww6E2

South African Naval Museum Website
http://simonstown.com/navalmuseum/
South African Naval Museum Map
https://goo.gl/maps/CcDLpikE7Q12

The Springbok Experience Rugby Museum Website
https://www.facebook.com/SpringbokRugbyMuseum/
The Springbok Experience Rugby Museum Map
https://goo.gl/maps/ABTGR13xevv

The University of Cape Town Website
http://www.uct.ac.za/
The University of Cape Town Map
https://goo.gl/maps/DpvXoxrKHRB2

The Green Point Lighthouse Map
https://goo.gl/maps/7aFGRJcpVHu
Khayelitsha Township Tour Website
http://www.nomvuyos-tours.co.za/

Parliament Buildings Website
http://www.parliament.gov.za/live/content.php?Category_ID=32
Parliament Buildings Map
https://goo.gl/maps/qNtK2fgMs882

Something Scenic

Cape Town is arguably the most beautiful city in the world. The variety and natural beauty that you get in the city is something that make Cape Town very Special. You can be in the middle of the city to have coffee and then 30 minutes later be in Constantia drinking some of best wine in the world. Let's take a look at a few scenic drives around Cape Town.

Constantia Wine Route Website
http://constantiawineroute.com/
Constantia Map
https://goo.gl/maps/7zYgKx8YNeK2

Llandudno Map
https://goo.gl/maps/9oTQSsj62192

Sandy Bay Map
https://goo.gl/maps/qa6hntJYbaT2

Chapman's Peak and Noordhoek Website
http://www.chapmanspeakdrive.co.za/
Chapman's Peak and Noordhoek Map
https://goo.gl/maps/MpNwbRBFhbH2

City Sightseeing Bus Tours Website
https://www.citysightseeing.co.za/cape-town
City Sightseeing Bus Tours Map
https://goo.gl/maps/KtDMnzVG4Qv

Beaches

The beaches of Cape Town has the reputation as some of the best in the world.Again the variety of Cape Town beaches gives you a unique experience.You can be in the Indian ocean, surfing and 30 minutes later have a barbeque on the beach next to the Atlantic ocean.

Clifton Beach Map
https://goo.gl/maps/Sy4FN79KYVm

Camps Bay Map
https://goo.gl/maps/9pMi2uDZdyE2

Melkbosstrand Map
https://goo.gl/maps/PCjbf4xfKh92

Muizenberg Map
https://goo.gl/maps/etM6VHqfZZR2

Kommetjie Map
https://goo.gl/maps/PMqTRdttskT2

Bikini Beach Map
https://goo.gl/maps/nQGzjJvGSTE2

Restaurants

Cape Town will not disappoint when it comes to food.And if you are a foodie and want to experience something special then Cape Town will provide just that.Cape Town will give you a global culinary experience you will never forget.

Mzoli's Website
https://www.facebook.com/Mzolis-Meat-Gugulethu-
Cape-Town-280620193730/
Mzoli's Map
https://goo.gl/maps/u4CGs8tCcoC2

Gold Restaurant Website
http://www.goldrestaurant.co.za/
Gold Restaurant Map
https://goo.gl/maps/jni1FzpzJvj

Addis in Cape Website
http://www.addisincape.co.za/
Addis in Cape Map

https://goo.gl/maps/vg8VNTdu4im

Beijing Opera Website
https://www.facebook.com/TheBeijingOpera/
Beijing Opera Map
https://goo.gl/maps/19swy1aheQT2

Beluga Website
http://www.beluga.co.za/
Beluga Map
https://goo.gl/maps/XnqRaWpzBY82

Izakaya Matsur Website
http://www.izakayamatsuri.com/
Izakaya Matsur Map
https://goo.gl/maps/eDgA28pVqm42

Bistrot Bizerca Website
http://www.bizerca.com/
Bistrot Bizerca Map
https://goo.gl/maps/kWoTLy3Hswv

95 Keerom Website
http://95keerom.com/
95 Keerom Map
https://goo.gl/maps/qgcP8Zvs9pt

Posticino Website
http://posticino.co.za/
Posticino Map
https://goo.gl/maps/yq3nbotootD2

Hemelhuijs Website

http://www.hemelhuijs.co.za/
Hemelhuijs Map
https://goo.gl/maps/QMrHvKA2F632

Col'cacchio Camps Bay Website
http://www.colcacchio.co.za/
Col'cacchio Camps Bay Map
https://goo.gl/maps/9y56AEfL5hq

Coffee

Coffee is part of the culture in Cape Town, and there are many coffee shops scattered around the city.Cape Town is going through a bit of a coffee revolution, and you will find some of the best coffee experiences in the world.

RCaffé Lomg Street Website
http://www.rcaffe.biz/
RCaffé Lomg Street Map
https://goo.gl/maps/kgSoSxo91yq

Mischu: The Coffee Showroom Website
http://www.mischu.co.za/
Mischu: The Coffee Showroom Map
https://goo.gl/maps/Uu1fVUcKAzK2

Molten Toffee Website
https://www.facebook.com/moltentoffee/
Molten Toffee Map
https://goo.gl/maps/Q9P1Xw3yjnD2

Tribe Coffee Café Website
http://www.tribecoffee.co.za/cafes/
Tribe Coffee Café Map
https://goo.gl/maps/tcRd5G8Hdrx

Jason Bakery Website
http://www.jasonbakery.com/
Jason Bakery Map
https://goo.gl/maps/wk16nRtUZKp
Truth Coffee Website (one of best in world)
http://www.truthcoffee.com/
Truth Coffee One of the best article website
http://www.telegraph.co.uk/food-and-drink/drinks/the-worlds-best-coffee-shops/
Truth Coffee Map
https://goo.gl/maps/w2aJz89AhF82

Bars and Clubs

Cape Town is well known for its dynamic nightlife that kicks off early and end late.Getting around the city at night is easy and affordable by taxi.Uber is a very convenient way to hop from one bar or club to the next.

The Waiting Room Website

https://www.facebook.com/WaitingRoomCT
The Waiting Room Map
https://goo.gl/maps/yXpRJuvDUAL2

The Foreign Exchange Bar in Cape Town Website
http://theforeignexchange.co.za/
The Foreign Exchange Bar in Cape Town Map
https://goo.gl/maps/2QQhvft4NDS2

Beerhouse in Cape Town Website
http://www.beerhouse.co.za/
Beerhouse in Cape Town Map
https://goo.gl/maps/1V854msGkdn

Tjing Tjing Rooftop Bar Website
http://www.tjingtjing.co.za/tjingtjing/
Tjing Tjing Rooftop Bar Map
https://goo.gl/maps/1mfpc5wwim32
The Dubliner Website
http://dubliner.co.za/
The Dubliner Map
https://goo.gl/maps/oEccvdWRY6z

The Shack Website
https://www.facebook.com/The-Shack-224820714213606/
The Shack Map
https://goo.gl/maps/cuf9hzadwV72

Rafiki's Website
http://rafikis.co.za/
Rafiki's Cape Town
https://goo.gl/maps/ZUxvtGP41nu

Alexander Bar and Café Website
https://alexanderbar.co.za/
Alexander Bar and Café Map
https://goo.gl/maps/k66ZfmopVMw

Buena Vista Social Café Website
http://www.buenavista.co.za/gallery/green-point/
Buena Vista Social Café Map
https://goo.gl/maps/YB8hcaEHNRU2

Cartel Bar Website
https://www.facebook.com/cartelcapetown/timeline
Cartel Bar Map
https://goo.gl/maps/nbZp6psziBn
La Vie Website
https://www.facebook.com/laviecapetown
La Vie Map
https://goo.gl/maps/XVXFU7r1V5A2

Dune's Beach Bar and Restaurant Website
http://www.dunesrestaurant.co.za/
Dune's Beach Bar and Restaurant Map
https://goo.gl/maps/PGEZJuEghds

Blue Peter Hotel BarWebsite
http://www.bluepeter.co.za/dining.html
Blue Peter Hotel Bar Map
https://goo.gl/maps/fBqB9u3AzkA2

Café Caprice Website
http://cafecaprice.co.za/
Café Caprice Map
https://goo.gl/maps/W9p8c9Mhc1K2

Fireman's Arms Website
http://firemansarms.co.za/
Fireman's Arms Map
https://goo.gl/maps/GPeVwsC7hdz

La Med Website (The Bungalow)
http://www.thebungalow.co.za/
La Med Map
https://goo.gl/maps/qBLV6kXSW9C2

Neighbourhood Restaurant, Bar & Lounge Website
http://www.goodinthehood.co.za/
Neighbourhood Restaurant, Bar & Lounge Map
https://goo.gl/maps/sVVgm5vNnB12

Perserverance Tavern Website
http://www.perseverancetavern.co.za/
Perserverance Tavern Map
https://goo.gl/maps/pHnXWVV1WQM2

Bascule Website
http://www.basculebar.com/
Bascule Map
https://goo.gl/maps/WwMoS2onwLU2

Decodance Website (Night Club)
https://www.facebook.com/clubdecodance
Decodance Map
https://goo.gl/maps/rHL4yLTbBPx

The Assembly Website
http://theassembly.co.za/

The Assembly Map
https://goo.gl/maps/8UKbLzoJngr

Chez Ntemba Nightclub Website
https://www.facebook.com/Chez-Ntemba-VIP-Club-Cape-Town-549783715051803/
Chez Ntemba Nightclub Map
https://goo.gl/maps/uzyAaM7wDf72

Hotels

Cape Town has hotels to suit any budget.I have put together a combination of budget and more upscale hotels to give you an idea of what is available in the city.

City Lodge VA Waterfront Website
https://clhg.com/hotels/180/City-Lodge-Hotel-Victoria-and-Alfred-Waterfront-
City Lodge VA Waterfront Map
https://goo.gl/maps/Ryd2zbEWccP2

51 on Camps Bay Website
http://www.51oncampsbay.com/
51 on Camps Bay Map
https://goo.gl/maps/exfGZVqAnjx

Cape Cadogan Website
http://www.capecadogan.co.za/
Cape Cadogan Map
https://goo.gl/maps/TvMkZHmFufF2

Ashanti Lodge and Travel Centre Website
http://ashanti.co.za/
Ashanti Lodge and Travel Centre Map
https://goo.gl/maps/aDRvQnroNYH2

Four Rosmead 'boutique guesthouse' Website
http://fourrosmead.com/
Four Rosmead 'boutique guesthouse' Map
https://goo.gl/maps/Kyd7LuMiwzr
Daddy Long Legs Website
http://daddylonglegs.co.za/arthotel/
Daddy Long Legs Map
https://goo.gl/maps/YZmUdr3iKaS2

The Hout Bay Hideaway Website
http://www.houtbay-hideaway.com/
The Hout Bay Hideaway Map
https://goo.gl/maps/byxTSsrnMdE2

Cape Heritage Hotel Website
http://capeheritage.co.za/
Cape Heritage Hotel Map
https://goo.gl/maps/fzqGHdsyKVE2

African Villa Hotel Website
http://www.anafricanvilla.co.za/
African Villa Hotel Map
https://goo.gl/maps/g2tEWeV5RhG2
Chartfield Guesthouse Website
http://www.chartfield.co.za/
Chartfield Guesthouse Map
https://goo.gl/maps/zXSnGLN5aAS2

Sea Five Website
http://www.seafive.co.za/
Sea Five Map
https://goo.gl/maps/Q2Te5kxZ2TK2

Mount Nelson Website
http://www.belmond.com/mount-nelson-hotel-cape-town/
Mount Nelson Map
https://goo.gl/maps/iabsuycMcaQ2

Tintswalo Atlantic Hotel Website
http://www.tintswalo.com/atlantic/
Tintswalo Atlantic Hotel Map
https://goo.gl/maps/X5uSWnXvUL92

The Cape Grace Hotel & Spa Website
https://www.capegrace.com/#/en/Home
The Cape Grace Hotel & Spa Map
https://goo.gl/maps/nwdKWdUjcYH2
The Table Bay At The Waterfront Website
http://www.suninternational.com/table-bay/
The Table Bay At The Waterfront Map
https://goo.gl/maps/MsZQLNB4UZ52

One&Only Cape Town Website
https://www.oneandonlyresorts.com/one-and-only-cape-town-south-africa
One&Only Cape Town Map
https://goo.gl/maps/idWMsq5UaXB2

Shopping

Let's take a look at some of the best shopping areas of Cape Town. The VA Waterfront and Canal Walk will give you a world class shopping experience and you will find most popular brands in these shopping centers.

De Waterkant , Long Street and Woodstock will give you a unique Cape Town Shopping Experience that you will only find in a city like Cape Town.

Just take a walk down Long Street and then walk up into Kloof

Street. You will find something special in these two lovely streets.

De Waterkant Shopping Website 1
http://www.dewaterkant.com/attractions.html
De Waterkant Shopping Website 2
http://www.capequarter.co.za/
De Waterkant Map
https://goo.gl/maps/v9kNP6qSmCS2

Greenmarket Square Market Map
https://goo.gl/maps/vHAbkM1N8xp

Long Street Map
https://goo.gl/maps/Nrnz7jdKFJy

Kloof Street Map
https://goo.gl/maps/gnrYMoJfHYT2

Woodstock Exchange Website
http://woodstockexchange.co.za/
Woodstock Exchange Map
https://goo.gl/maps/x3ta4QQe3oy

VA Waterfront Website
http://www.waterfront.co.za/
VA Waterfront Map
https://goo.gl/maps/uJQ4PoiYQ942
Canal Walk Website
http://www.canalwalk.co.za/home.html
Canal Walk Map
https://goo.gl/maps/xpBW4TDGZJG2
Stellenbosch

Cape Town is very close to Stellenbosch, a town situated in the banks of the Eerste River and is known for its plentiful oak trees. According to history, these oak trees were planted by the town's founder, Simon Van der Stel in 1669. There are many vineyards in Stellenbosch, and also a lot of rugby activities available as it is the town's national sport.

The South African Wine Region is the oldest winemaking region in the world outside Europe.Stellenboch is the headquarters of the wine industry in South Africa.Stellenboch is also filled with fantastic restaurants and art galleries.

Stellenbosch Map
https://goo.gl/maps/EX6h4yN7Yyj
Stellenbosch Travel Website
http://www.stellenbosch.travel/

Rust en Vrede Restaurant Website
http://rustenvrede.com/

Stellenbosch Wine Route
http://www.wineroute.co.za/

Jonkershoek Website
http://www.capenature.co.za/reserves/jonkershoek-nature-reserve/
Jonkershoek Map
https://goo.gl/maps/a1cRbD5yBem

Franschoek

Franschoek was originally settled in 1688 by 176 French Huguenot refugees that were fleeing France.

The valley town of Franschoek has a facinating history and has some of the best winefarms in the country.Franschoek is also home to Reuben's, considered as one of the Top 50 Best Restaurants in the World by S. Pellegrino.

Franschoek Map
https://goo.gl/maps/5faaCCzmjWA2
Franschoek Website
http://www.franschhoek.co.za/

Franschoek Wine Valley Website
http://franschhoek.org.za/
Reuben's Restaurant Website
http://reubens.co.za/
Robertson Wine Valley

Robertson is a Town about 1 and half hour drive outside of Cape Town.It is home to some great winefarms and is known for its natural beauty.

Robertson Wine Valley Website
http://www.robertsonwinevalley.com/
Robertson Wine Valley Map
https://goo.gl/maps/rCRvjWANBRz

Hermanus

Meanwhile, there's also Hermanus where you could go whale watching during spring and summer. Hermanus is also home to the South African Whale Festival. This is also considered a great retirement town and has one of the highest plant diversities in the world, that's why it's deemed as the Cape's Floristic Region. You could also visit the famous Grotto Beach in the said area.

Hermanus Map
https://goo.gl/maps/K2NbZ7qmbq72
Hermanus Travel Website
http://www.hermanustourism.info/

Hermanus Whale Watching Website
http://www.hermanus.co.za/whales

Grootbos Private Nature Reserve Website
http://www.grootbos.com/en/home
Grootbos Private Nature Reserve Map
https://goo.gl/maps/Bxa3KrAqxx62

Fernkloof Nature Reserve Website
http://fernkloof.com/
Fernkloof Nature Reserve Map
https://goo.gl/maps/RSJS92qPCFo
Grabouw
And then there's Grabouw, known as the Elgin Valley's prime
commercial center. This is the largest fruit exporting area in all
of Africa. While there, you could also visit the Hottentots Holland
Mountains and the Biosphere Reserve, so you could learn more about
nature. You could also join the annual Elgin Festival to taste wines,
fruits, and see vast flower displays that would leave you in awe!

There's also such a place called Grabouw Suicide Gorge, which as
scary and dark as it sounds is actually just a wet hiking place. Apart
from the hike, it will also allow you to see waterfalls and a great canyon
sanctuary that would take your breath away!
Grabouw Map
https://goo.gl/maps/RgaxmjxHtdy
Grabouw(Elgin Valley) Website
http://www.elginvalley.co.za/Default.aspx
Grabouw Suicide Gorge Website 1
http://www.frixionadventures.co.za/adventure-tourism/suicide-
gorge.htm
Grabouw Suicide Gorge Website 2
http://www.capenature.co.za/reserves/hottentots-holland-nature-
reserve/

Grabouw Suicide Gorge Map

https://goo.gl/maps/MtWyJpDPjD82

West Coast

Langebaan

In the West Coast, there's Langebaan with its famous Langebaan Lagoon that dates back up to 500,000 years ago—giving it a vast history, and making it one of the most important places in South Africa.

Today, bird-watching is prominent in Langebaan, with over 300 species of birds in the area! The Spring Flower Season also proves to be busy, and you can also spend time in the white sand beaches surrounding the land, especially in the Club Mykonos Resort. The Langebaan Mussel Festival also takes place during the first week of October.Langebaan is home to one of the best Seafood Restaurants in the world called Die Strandloper.This restaurant is on the beach, and you will have an amazing experience.

Langebaan Website

http://capewestcoastpeninsula.co.za/langebaan/

Langebaan Map

https://goo.gl/maps/i5GY73Epptw

Die Starndloper Restaurant

http://www.strandloper.com/

Die Strandloper Map

https://goo.gl/maps/sX6aVQZo7gS2

Paternoster

And of course, there's also Paternoster, one of the oldest fishing villages in the West Coast of South Africa. According to legend, the place got its name from Pater Noster (The Lord's Prayer), as this is what old fisherfolk used to pray during thunderstorms while fishing in the sea.Remember the visit the Paternoster Hotel and have a drink at the legendary Paternoster Hotel Bar.

Today, you can visit the Cape Columbine Lighthouse, which has been around since 1936 and see the Nature Reserve also in the said area.

During spring, you could visit Namaqualand as it becomes a floral paradise, and you can also go kite surfing, snorkeling, or kayaking Cold—if you feel like it!

Paternoster Website
http://www.paternoster.co.za/
Paternoster Hotel Map
https://goo.gl/maps/smfDZ7ZrsRu
Paternoster Hotel Website
http://www.paternosterhotel.co.za/
Paternoster Map
https://goo.gl/maps/7pc2bn9HLQz

Cape Columbine Lighthouse Map
https://goo.gl/maps/bmBAickYGH52
Namaqualand Website
http://www.namaqualand.com/
Namaqualand Map

https://goo.gl/maps/u4eFM81gyxq

The Garden Route

The Garden Route is known as one of the most beautiful areas in the world.There's also the Garden Route and it's ecologically diverse, verdant vegetation. Garden Route also serves as home to Nature's Valley, Plettenberg Bay, Knysna, and George, which is known as the Garden Route's largest administrative centre.

The Garden Route is situated between the Indian Ocean and the Tsitsikamma and Outenquia Mountains. While there, you could visit the Fairy Knowe Station, the Tsitsikamma National Park, and the Garden Route Vineyard.

The Garden Route.Remeber to go Bungy jumping at Bloukrans Bridge, it is the higest commercial jump in the world, it has a 250 meters drop.George is home to world class golf Courses like Fan Court, where the Presidents Cup was hosted a few years ago .You can Fly into George from most major cities and explore the Garden Route from George if your time is limited.Try Airlink or Kulula Airlines.

George Airport Website

http://www.airports.co.za/airports/george-airport
George Map
https://goo.gl/maps/ZnP1ZPfp19u
George Fancourt Golf Website
http://www.fancourt.co.za/en/home/
George City Website
http://www.georgeinfo.org/

Knysna Map
https://goo.gl/maps/wdUfYfdReKL2
Knysna Website
http://www.visitknysna.co.za/

Plettenberg Bay Map
https://goo.gl/maps/trLjzit4UCD2
Plettenberg Bay Website
http://www.plett-tourism.co.za/

Tsitsikamma National Park Website
http://www.tsitsikamma.info/

Bloukrans Bungy Jump Website
https://www.faceadrenalin.com/
Bloukrans Bungy Jump Map
https://goo.gl/maps/c39hzK99m6m

- While in the Western Cape, you should at least try doing one of the following:
- Check out the famous Table Mountain.
- Sit down and relax at the Table Mountain National Park to enjoy picturesque views!
- Walk along the Cape of Good Hope to frolic in the sea, or just walk around the shore.
- Go on a Wine Tasting Tour at either Cape Town Wine or Cape Convoy. The Western Cape has some of the best vineyards around!
- Ride the cable cars at Table Mountain Aerial Cable-way—you'd definitely feel like you're on top of the world!
- Check out Boulders Beach, swim, or just see if you can get a sight of the adorable African Penguins!
- Check out Cape Point Lighthouse, and see the place where the two oceans meet! This is said to be one of the most spectacular views of all!
- Visit the Cango Caves to see all-natural, uninhabited caves!
- Visit the Garden Route National Park that has lovely mountains

and bays, and with over a thousand varieties of flowers!
· Visit the Langa Township, which is the cultural town of the Western Cape to learn more about the province's rich history and culture!

Cape Point Website
http://capepoint.co.za/
Cape Point Map
https://goo.gl/maps/kWXLbTRDXE92

Table Mountain Website
http://www.tablemountain.net/
Table Mountain Map
https://goo.gl/maps/pqri17UceB92
Table Mountain National Park Website
https://www.sanparks.org/parks/table_mountain/

Boulders Beach Map
https://goo.gl/maps/iUBCH7vgtdN2

Cango Caves Website
http://www.cango-caves.co.za/
Cango Caves Map
https://goo.gl/maps/ooLcPZfi9dS2

Garden Route National Park Website
https://www.sanparks.org/parks/garden_route/
Garden Route National Park Map
https://goo.gl/maps/UQQZPWwP3JP2

Safety in Cape Town City Website
http://www.capetownsafety.com/safety-at-night/

7

The Best of the Eastern Cape

Next up is the Eastern Cape, which became an independent province in 1994, just like the Western Cape. This serves as the traditional home to the Xhosas, and has also been home for Nelson Mandela.

The late President Nelson Mandela used to live in Qunu, a small rural village in the Eastern Cape, most specifically in the Mvezo Village. His father was then deposed as Qunu's Chief, and according to Mandela, Qunu is home to his happiest memories, even talking about it in his autobiography, Long Way to Freedom. Mandela's remains is now buried in a spot he selected in Qunu, after being exhumed from Mvezo.

Eastern Cape Map
https://goo.gl/maps/wJSzcD3pZ652
Qunu Map
https://goo.gl/maps/PrB9dSktCvQ2
Port Elizabeth
Speaking of Nelson Mandela, you also have the Nelson Mandela Bay, which was named after the former President and Apartheid Leader. This is now an administrative area that covers Port Elizabeth, Despatch, and Uitenhage.

Port Elizabeth has also been around since the 1820s and is considered as one of the largest cities in South Africa, and was once home to British Settlers. In 2010, the Port Elizabeth Harbor was upgraded to make way for the 2010 FIFA World Cup, making the waterfront, even more, majestic to the eyes of many! The Nelson Mandela Bay Stadium was also established.

Port Elizabeth Website
http://www.nmbt.co.za/
Port Elizabeth Map
https://goo.gl/maps/oT6ZXKCMMUK2
Shamwari Game Reserve Website
http://www.shamwari.com/
Shamwari Game Reserve Map
https://goo.gl/maps/BhHtRFYRc1N2
Addo Elephant National Park Website
https://www.sanparks.org/parks/addo/
Addo Elephant National Park Map
https://goo.gl/maps/q66gCnAx7c22
Jeffrey's Bay
Meanwhile, there's also Jeffrey's Bay, which is known as the Surfing Capital of South Africa. The place was named after a man named Jeffrey who built up a store in the area back in 1849 with his partner,

Glendinnings. In the 70s, Jeffrey's Bay became a prominent hippie hangout, and is now one of the fastest expanding fishing areas in the world!If you have time, check out St Francis Bay and Baviaanskloof Nature Reserve.

Jeffrey's Bay Website
http://www.jeffreysbaytourism.org/
Jeffrey's Bay Map
https://goo.gl/maps/YfBKJRtgjmN2
St Francis Bay Website
http://stfrancisbay.co.za/
St Francis Bay Map
https://goo.gl/maps/nx6iV24qytu
Baviaanskloof Website
http://www.baviaanskloof.net/
Baviaanskloof Info Website
http://www.baviaanskloofinfo.co.za/
Baviaanskloof Map
https://goo.gl/maps/vcDPVT8mseu

Graaf Reinet

There's also Graaf Reinet, which is the 4th oldest town in South Africa. It is home to several tourist attractions, such as The Karoo Architecture, The Agave Distillery, the Reinet House Museum, Camdeboo National Park, the Valley of Desolation, and the Drostdy Hotel, amongst others.If you have extra time, check out the Owl House.

Graaf Reinet Website
http://www.graaffreinet.com/
Graaf Reinet Map
https://goo.gl/maps/x5NephPN5b22
Camdeboo National Park Website
https://www.sanparks.org/parks/camdeboo/
Camdeboo National Park Map
https://goo.gl/maps/Kf3MGemUGJS2
The Valley of Desolation Map
https://goo.gl/maps/piagmmsBKbu
The Reinet House Museum Website
http://www.graaffreinetmuseums.co.za/reinet_house.html
The Reinet House Museum Map
https://goo.gl/maps/Em86Tqsikkz
Drostdy Hotel Website
http://www.graaffreinet.com/accom/drostdy/
Drostdy Hotel Map
https://goo.gl/maps/5uBu7HMJfAK2

The Owl House Website
http://theowlhouse.co.za/
The Owl House Map
https://goo.gl/maps/UJXwdSKVWJs
Wild Coast Region

You also have the Wild Coast Region, which is close to the border of KwaZulu-Natal and is the traditional home of the Xhosas. There are lots of rivers, cliffs, and waterfalls in the area, making it one of the most scenic places in all of Africa. Here, you could visit the Inkwenkwezi Private Game Reserve and spend some time with the animals and with nature, in general!

Wild Coast Website
http://www.wildcoast.co.za/
Wild Coast Map
https://goo.gl/maps/VnUtfTrztdy
Inkwenkwezi Private Game Reserve Website
http://www.nature-reserve.co.za/inkwenkwezi-nature-reserve.html

Inkwenkwezi Private Game Reserve Map
https://goo.gl/maps/NusU6i6PCeB2
Top 10 Things to Do:

- Check out the Shamwari Game Reserve to see lions and cubs in their natural habitat. This would definitely make you feel one with nature!
- Visit the Addo National Park where you could see lots of elephants and get to rediscover yourself a bit! It's definitely a great sanctuary!
- Go to the Mountain Zebra National Park. Enjoy the great landscape and see zebras in their natural habitat, having fun and being adorable!
- Visit Kragga Kama Game Park where you could eat with giraffes around, and just breathe in the fresh air and enjoy what nature gave you!
- Check out the Harrison Hope Wine Estate.

- Visit the Velvet Jazz Lounge, listen to music, enjoy wine and cheese and other sumptuous gourmet meals!
- Have fun at the Boardwalk Casino and Entertainment World!
- Visit the South African Marine Rehabilitation and Education Centre. Here, you can learn more about fish and African Penguins, amongst other animals, so your respect for them could increase and you could enjoy your time in South Africa more!
- Visit the Owl House Museum—a hauntingly beautiful and picturesque museum and inn for you to stay in!
- And, visit the Valley of Desolation—which has one of the most spectacular views in all of the Eastern Cape!

Mountain Zebra National Park Website
https://www.sanparks.org/parks/mountain_zebra/
Mountain Zebra National Park Map
https://goo.gl/maps/HTH9j2f3rnq
Kragga Kama Game Park Website
http://www.kraggakamma.co.za/
Kragga Kama Game Park Map
https://goo.gl/maps/wnxtgJGyCSy
Harrison Hope Wine Estate Website
http://www.harrisonhope.com/
Harrison Hope Wine Estate Map
https://goo.gl/maps/7NHQzMnJPy62
Velvet Jazz Lounge Website
http://www.thevelvetjazzlounge.co.za/
Velvet Jazz Lounge Map
https://goo.gl/maps/HuPfzwgBLdT2
Boardwalk Casino and Entertainment World Website
http://www.suninternational.com/boardwalk/
Boardwalk Casino and Entertainment World Map
https://goo.gl/maps/oQouyJpTcgm
South African Marine Rehabilitation and Education Centre Website

http://www.samrec.org.za/

8

The Best of the Northern Cape

Northern Cape

Upington

Next, you have the Northern Cape. This is considered as the most sparsely populated province in South Africa and is home to many amazing tourist attractions, such as the Kgalagadi National Park close to Upington. This is a wildlife reserve and conservation center, and straddles the border between Botswana and South Africa. Here, you'll find Hyenas, African Leopards, Namibian Cheetahs, and Kalahari Lions with their majestic black manes! There are also over 200 species of birds in the park, including sanctuary birds, buzzards, and eagles, amongst others!

Northern Cape Map
https://goo.gl/maps/dxMiigUKk6p
Upington Website
http://www.upington.com/
Upington Map
https://goo.gl/maps/oz8RxYrXTGD2
Kgalagadi National Park Website
https://www.sanparks.org/parks/kgalagadi/
Kgalagadi National Park Map
https://goo.gl/maps/dxmZavv3jEL2

The Augrabies Falls National Park is also located in Upington, and has been around since 1966. One of the most enchanting facts about the park is the Quiver Tree or the Giant Aloe that has a lot of alluvial

75

deposits that you won't find anywhere else in the world.

The Augrabies Falls National Park Website
https://www.sanparks.org/parks/augrabies/
The Augrabies Falls National Park Map
https://goo.gl/maps/6a6nT87fDa72

Kimberley

Kimberley is the capital of the Northern Cape and is home to the Big Hole, formerly called the Mine Museum. This serves as both museum and recreated townscape that would help you learn more about the rich culture and history of the Northern Cape, thanks to a vast collection of artifacts from the early days of the Cape! Kimberley is also home to the Halfway House and The Star, these two pubs are some of the oldest bars in the country.

Kimberley Website 1
http://www.kimberley.co.za/
Kimberley Website 2
http://kimberleytourism.co.za/
Kimberley Map
https://goo.gl/maps/WqRvsVvjqE12
The Big Hole Website
http://thebighole.co.za/
The Big Hole Map
https://goo.gl/maps/eeSegUg6tTD2
Halfway House Website
http://www.kimberley.co.za/city/the-halfway-house-pub-the-half/
Halfway House Map
https://goo.gl/maps/jRFDHxdRe9m
The Star Website
http://www.kimberley.co.za/city/star-of-the-west-pub-restaurant/
The Star Map
https://goo.gl/maps/4iPBLvh5e2M2
Protea Hotel Map

https://goo.gl/maps/fvr9S8KR4TM2

Aside from that, you can also visit the Honored Dead Memorial—a testament to those who gave up their lives during the Anglo-Boer War, the Concentration Camp Memorial, the Cenotaph—which was intended to commemorate lives lost during the First World War, the Henrietta Stockdale Statue and the Burger Monument.

Honored Dead Memorial

http://www.kimberley.org.za/monuments-and-memorials/

Wildebeest Kuli Rock Art Centre Website

http://www.wildebeestkuil.itgo.com/

Wildebeest Kuli Rock Art Centre Map

https://goo.gl/maps/2zNyzqV4L212

Hopetown

The Northern Cape is also home to Hopetown, which is found at the edge of Great Karoo and where the Great Diamond of Africa was discovered. Hopetown is also where you could visit the Doornbult

Concentration Camp Memorials, another remnant of the historic Anglo-Boer War.

Doornbult Concentration Camp Memorials

http://www.doornbult.com/

Hopetown Map

https://goo.gl/maps/ftVr75KUL6r

Sutherland

Then, you have Sutherland, where you could find the South African Large Telescope (SALT), which boasts of 91 Hexagonal Mirror Segments that enables spectroscopy, polarimetric analysis, and space imaging! In 2005, the full mirror first light was added to the telescope, making the experience of viewing through it a more magnificent experience! This is considered as the Star of the West!

Sutherland Website

http://www.discoversutherland.co.za/

Sutherland Map

https://goo.gl/maps/qhCtx7gsqC62

South African Large Telescope (SALT)
http://www.salt.ac.za/
South African Large Telescope (SALT) Map
https://goo.gl/maps/1utD6S4iq672
Top 10 Things to Do:

- Visit the Kgalagadi Transfrontier Park, and see animals such as lions, buffalos, and more! It would be best to visit during the summer, though, because storms are prevalent in the area other times of the year. It is the "Palace of Storms", after all.
- Check out the Augrabies Falls National Park where rainbows are pretty much normal!
- Check out the Big Hole Kimberley, a man-made hole that looks so natural, it's hard to believe that it's actually man-made!
- Enjoy time with the colorful and amazing flowers at the Namaqua National Park.
- Visit the Southern Africa Large Telescope and try to tap into your inner astronaut! It's also best visited after a road trip in The Karoo.

- Visit Bezazel Wine and Brandy Estate—not only will you get to drink amazing wines, you'd also learn more about the history of the winery, and the Northern Cape!
- Check out the Wildebeest Kuli Rock Art Centre, which is one of the best rock hilltop sites in all of South Africa.
- Visit the Hamtam Botanical Garden and be one with nature even more!
- Pay respects to the memories of people

Bezazel Wine and Brandy Estate Website
https://www.bezalel.co.za/
Bezazel Wine and Brandy Estate Map
https://goo.gl/maps/6XwExzfkqms

9

The Best of the Free State

Free State

Next on the list is the Free State. Pasturelands and flat, grassy plains are prominent in the area, and is also close to the foothills of Maluti and Drakensberg. It is one of the only four original African Provinces that didn't get unnecessary changes, and has since been a premier province. It is also known as the breadbasket of South Africa because it's able to produce around 70% of the country's grains!

Free State Map
https://goo.gl/maps/oRWhdVdY3v82
Bloemfontein
Its capital, Bloemfontein is known as South Africa's judicial capital, and one of South Africa's three main capitals. Blomfontein is also known as the City of Roses because of the popular Rose Festival that's held in the area, as well as the fact that there are so many flowers around. It also was a big part of the Anglo-Boer War, making it one of the most historical places in South Africa.
Bloemfontein Website
http://www.bloemfonteintourism.co.za/
Bloemfontein Map
https://goo.gl/maps/HZQFm8xicwm
In Bloemfontein, you could find the Raadsal, also known as the statue of Christian de Wet, a popular figure of the war. Apart from that, you could also spend time with the cheetahs at Bainsvlei, check out the Bagamoya Wildlife Estate where you could see warhogs, adorable tigers, and ostriches, visit Oliewenhuis Art Gallery, check out the Botanical Garden, as well as the Anglo-Boer and National Museum so you could learn more about what happened back in the olden days.
The Raadsal Map
https://goo.gl/maps/GMdhhLEmQi22
Bainsvlei Cheetah Experience Website
http://www.cheetahexperience.com/
Bainsvlei Cheetah Experience Map
https://goo.gl/maps/CepEmZyLANP2
Bagamoya Wildlife Estate Website
http://www.bagamoyawildlifeestate.co.za/
Bagamoya Wildlife Estate Map
https://goo.gl/maps/qYuou4RW9nL2
Oliewenhuis Art Gallery Website
https://www.facebook.com/OliewenhuisArtMuseum/
Oliewenhuis Art Gallery Map

https://goo.gl/maps/8ShTZWtDFXs
Botanical Garden Map
https://goo.gl/maps/AMVSNHWTSxH2

Aside from that, you should savor the beauty of the Free State more by visiting the Golden Gate Highlands National Park to spend time with the zebras , check out Lionsrock Big Cat Sanctuary which is known as one of the best day outing destinations in South Africa, visit the Dell Cheetah Center before going to the Free State National Botanical Garden to rest and reflect a bit, check out the Naval Hill Planetarium, spend time at the Gariep Dam Nature Reserve, and appreciate art at the Gallery on Lavesieur. After that, you could plan a trip to the lovely town **Clarens**.Rent a car and take a trip to this picturesque town.Another town that is worth visiting is **Parys**.In Parys, you can go skydiving and make your trip, even more, memorable.

Golden Gate Highlands National Park Website
https://www.sanparks.org/parks/golden_gate/
Golden Gate Highlands National Park Map
https://goo.gl/maps/2QNjRvBugXM2
Lionsrock Big Cat Sanctuary Website
http://www.lionsrock.org/

Lionsrock Big Cat Sanctuary Map
https://goo.gl/maps/x1zKnBoE2hD2
Clarens Website
http://clarens.co.za/
Clarens Map
https://goo.gl/maps/njibZZh1RVm
Parys Website
http://www.parys.co.za/
Parys Map
https://goo.gl/maps/PVRj7SHHNcG2
Parys Skydiving Website
http://www.skydiveparys.co.za/
Parys Skydiving Map
https://goo.gl/maps/TQFSzuLbqQv
Top 10 Things to Do:

· While in the Free State, don't forget to:
· Visit the Oliewenhuis Art Museum, where you could have some

serenity while having picnic or even feel like you're attending a wedding of some sorts.

- Visit the Clarens Brewery, especially on hot days as they serve the best, coldest beers in town.
- Check out the Bagamoya Wildlife Estate, get close to the lions, and enjoy fantastic food from the locals.
- Be one with nature at the Golden Gate Highlands National Park. This has amazing sights, and a load of zebras for you to see!
- See the lovely, brave cheetahs at the Dell Cheetah Centre—this is said to be such an out of this world experience that you definitely shouldn't miss!
- Visit the National Museum to learn more about the history of the Free State.
- Enjoy flora and fauna at the Free State Botanical Garden, walk on bridges, and feel the cool water at your feet!
- Visit the Gariep Dam Nature Reserve—a breathtaking adventure that you'd always remember!
- Go skydiving at Parys—conquer your fears!

Gariep Dam Nature Reserve Website
http://www.gariepdam.co.za/gariepdam/NatureReserve/
Gariep Dam Website
http://www.gariepdam.com/
Gariep Dam Map
https://goo.gl/maps/tayo5bqzSfv

10

The Best of Kwazulu-Natal

Then, there's Kwazulu-Natal, also known as the Garden Province of South Africa which has also been created back in 1994 after the traditional Zula state was merged with the old Natal province.Kwazulu-Natal is next to the warm Indian Ocean, and actually shares borders with Lesotho, Swaziland, and Mozambique.The coastal areas has a subtropical climate.

Kwazulu-Natal Map
https://goo.gl/maps/NyqoDZVuVcF2
Durban

Durban is the largest city in Kwazulu-Natal and is known as one of the most populous metropolitan areas in South Africa, and is also the nation's busiest port. Durban is home to the Golden Mile where you could go on bike and segway trails. Aside from that, you could also spend some time in the uShaka Marine World where you could have fun swimming and enjoying water games as it is the largest water theme park in Africa, and is also home to one of the largest aquariums in the world!

Durban Website
http://www.durbanexperience.co.za/Pages/default.aspx
Durban Map
https://goo.gl/maps/xDZ993rJPiG2
uShaka Marine World Website
http://www.ushakamarineworld.co.za/
uShaka Marine World Map
https://goo.gl/maps/nCusXswygkr

Durban is also home to the iconic uMhlanga Beach and its Lighthouse, the International Convention Center, the Victoria Embankment(shopping area), and the Markets of Warwick.

Umhlanga Beach

http://www.umhlangatourism.co.za/

Umhlanga Beach Map

https://goo.gl/maps/QNq27dWxAPE2

Victoria Embankment Map

https://goo.gl/maps/aUFRpLUXEAk

Zululand District

Then, there's also Zululand, also known as Zululand District Municipality, which is also the seat of the Ulundi. In Zululand, you could learn more about the culture of Kwazulu-Natal in Nkwaleni Valley or hike in the Entumeni Nature Reserve. Apart from that, you could also check out the Emdoneni Cat Rehabilitation Centre or spend time with the animals at Ithala Game Reserve. Or, you could visit the Mtonjaneni Zulu Cultural Museum to feel like you're one of the people of KwaZulu-Natal. For your downtime, you could then fish at Papabeer Chapters or at the Pongola Game Reserve!

Zululand District Map
https://goo.gl/maps/qDRakwLsE9H2
Nkwaleni Valley Map
https://goo.gl/maps/MHGUFsnJj4P2
Entumeni Nature Reserve Website
http://www.birdlife.org.za/component/k2/item/207-sa066-entumeni-nature-reserve
Entumeni Nature Reserve Map
https://goo.gl/maps/aBihF92QVdp

There are also other important destinations in Kwazulu Natal that you have to see, and these include the Nambiti Game Reserve where you could easily spend time with a variety of wild animals, or stay at the lodge also located in the Reserve. Even Queen Elizabeth II used to do something like this shortly before her coronation in 1952!

Nambiti Game Reserve Website
http://www.nambiti.com/
Nambiti Game Reserve Map
https://goo.gl/maps/jyvfG9n2LBU2

Apart from that, you could also visit the Kwa Cheetah Breeding where you could check out baby cheetahs and see what is done to help them grow the right way. Most people who have been there saying that you definitely won't be disappointed, and it's such an unforgettable experience! Kwa Cheetah Breeding is located in Nambiti Game Reserve

Kwa Cheetah Breeding Website
https://www.facebook.com/kwacheetah/
Kwa Cheetah Breeding Map
https://goo.gl/maps/RVwj7izrYTH2

Then, you could check out the Drakensberg Mountains, a known world heritage site that offers scenic, spectacular views and where you could do the so-called Amphitheater Hike.

Drakensberg National Park Website
http://www.nature-reserve.co.za/drakensberg-national-park-travel-guide.html

Drakensberg National Park Map
https://goo.gl/maps/AASYhn8GBgs

Then, there's the African Bird of Prey Sanctuary where you could see eagles, ravens, owls, buzzards and other birds in a well-managed facility that's also near a café. Bunnies could also be fed nearby!

The Talana Museum is also nearby where you could find some artifacts from the Anglo-Boer War and spend time with fellow tourists!

Certainly, there is a lot to see in Kwazulu-Natal!

African Bird of Prey Sanctuary Website
http://africanraptor.co.za/

African Bird of Prey Sanctuary Map
https://goo.gl/maps/dyvLe3LPgzj

Talana Museum Website
http://www.battlefieldsroute.co.za/place/talana-battlefield-and-museum/

Talana Museum Map
https://goo.gl/maps/WF3BCe8nVJ52

Top 10 Things to Do:

- Visit iSiMalingaso Wetland Park, one of those little-known secrets to the rest of South Africa. Aside from wetlands, you'd also see Baboons, Vervet Monkeys and other animals and plants, too!
- Go to the UShaka Marine Park, an open-air water park where you could spend time with dolphins and African Penguins. There are three shows for you to watch here!
- Spend time with the animals at the Nambiti Game Reserve. You could stay at the Ndaka Lodge, and spend time with tigers, lions, and cheetahs later!
- Visit the Umhlanga Rocks, a sunny, exotic rocky beach where you could also feel one with nature!
- Visit the Durban Botanical Gardens and enjoy the sights of flora and fauna that will make you appreciate life even more!
- Have fun at Wet n' Wild, which has some of the best water slides anywhere in the world!
- Visit the Cathedral Peak Wine Estate, a spectacular wine reserve and vineyard that's also perfect as a wedding destination!
- Go taste some cheese at Underberg Cheesery—which has some of the best cheeses in all of Africa!
- Go on Shoreline Hippo and Croc Cruises to appreciate these feared animals!
- And finally, visit the Nelson Mandela Capture Site, and learn more about this important part of history, courtesy of two museums in the site.

Shoreline Hippo and Croc Cruises Website
http://www.heritagetoursandsafaris.com/hippo-crocodile-boat-safari-st-lucia/
Shoreline Hippo and Croc Cruises Map
https://goo.gl/maps/fBt6mNuuEjm
Nelson Mandela Capture Site Website
http://www.thecapturesite.co.za/

Nelson Mandela Capture Site Map
https://goo.gl/maps/YVLGvFDQjLJ2
Wet n' Wild Website
http://www.ushakamarineworld.co.za/wet-n-wild
Ndaka Lodge Website
http://www.ndaka.co.za/
Ndaka Lodge Map
https://goo.gl/maps/iBK3u138yR82
Cathedral Peak Wine Estate Website
http://cathpeakwines.com/

11

The Best of Gauteng

Gauteng

Gauteng was established after South Africa's first democratic elections in 1994 and was part of the old Transvaal Province. This was once called Pretoria-Witwatersrand-Vereeniging and is known as the smallest province in South Africa, but actually is home to Johannesburg, also known as the largest city in the nation, proving that big things really do come in small packages!

Gauteng Website
http://www.gauteng.net/
Gauteng Map
https://goo.gl/maps/5v8SX1FRH442

Johannesburg

Johannesburg is not only the largest, but also the wealthiest city in South Africa. This so happened because the town contains large gold reserves which has been discovered back in 1886, and has been a big part of gold and diamond trades since back in the day.

Johannesburg Map

https://goo.gl/maps/v24sAHD7Z922

While in Johannesburg, you could visit the Johannesburg Art Gallery where you could see figurative paintings, European, and African landscapes, and where you could visit the Market Theatre which used to host anti-apartheid plays. There are also lots of flea markets around where you could buy African Art and other souvenirs.

Johannesburg Art Gallery Website

http://www.gauteng.net/attractions/johannesburg_art_gallery/

Johannesburg Art Gallery Map

https://goo.gl/maps/yrzMfmQwNL62

Market Theatre Website

http://markettheatre.co.za/

Market Theatre Map
https://goo.gl/maps/JEx4kJHuc9P2
The Cradle of Humankind, a UNESCO World Heritage Site is also nearby and is home to fossils of the first adult Australopithecus Africanus, and near-complete skeletons of Australopetichine, or early men. This would help you understand the origin of human life in Africa even better.

While in Gauteng, you might also want to visit the Apartheid Museum in Pretoria. With recorded footage, you'd get to understand what the Apartheid Era is exactly about, and you could also take part in the audience of panels who talk about the said era, which is an important part of African History.

Cradle of Humankind, a UNESCO World Heritage Site Website
http://www.maropeng.co.za/
Cradle of Humankind, a UNESCO World Heritage Site Map
https://goo.gl/maps/bq1U19CTyTT2
Apartheid Museum Website
http://www.apartheidmuseum.org/
Apartheid Museum Map
https://goo.gl/maps/FvuTgyHLzsv
A lot of safaris are also around. Some of the best ones include Felleng Way Tours, Go Safari, Khakiweed Safari, and African Safari Guru Tours. These will help you be one with nature, enjoy time with wildlife, and get to understand this important aspect of South Africa while you're really out there, and not just reading about it.

Felleng Way Tours Website
http://www.fellengtours.com/daytours.html
Go Safari Website
http://www.gosafari.co.za/overnight_safaris/pilanesberg/safaris.html
Khakiweed Safari Website
http://www.khakiweed.co.za/index.htm
African Safari Guru Tours Website
http://www.africansafariguru.com/

There's also Constitution Hill and Voortrekker Monument, where you could somehow go back in time and learn more about the history of Africa—without being bored! The Lilesleaf Farm Museum is also a good way of connecting with locals and understanding the industry of Gauteng.

Constitution Hill Website
https://www.constitutionhill.org.za/
Constitution Hill Map
https://goo.gl/maps/RPC8ANWW8Mn
Lilesleaf Farm Museum Website
http://www.liliesleaf.co.za/
Lilesleaf Farm Museum Map
https://goo.gl/maps/YPrRfLvLE6Q2

A visit to the Southwestern Townships and the Lesedi Cultural Village would help you see Gauteng in different eyes. It's a thought-provoking experience that will help you appreciate yourself and your life more. The same goes for the Hector Pietersen Museum, which commemorates a turning point in the life of South African locales nationwide. Going on a Soweto Township tour is something very memorable.

Surely, a trip to Gauteng won't just be adventurous—it will also be educational and meaningful, too!

Soweto Township Tours Website
http://www.sowetotownshiptours.com/
Hector Pietersen Museum Website
http://www.soweto.co.za/html/p_hector.htm
Hector Pietersen Museum Map
https://goo.gl/maps/EWxQNUhPPFR2

Top 10 Things to Do:
- While in Gauteng, make sure to:
- Visit the Apartheid Museum to get a great understanding of the Apartheid Era, one of the most life-changing factors in South Africa. It's touching and informative at the same time.

- Go to Horseback Africa and try to see the town while riding a healthy horse!
- Visit the Voortrekker Monument, and get back in time a bit by stepping back and being a part of history yourself!
- Check out the Walter Sisulu Botanical Garden. Not only is it one of the most beautiful gardens in the world, but you could also go on a trail run, making it an adventure of its own!
- Visit the Mandela House to learn more about the late, great Nelson Mandela!
- Have fun at the Honeydew Mazes where you could go on your very own treasure hunt!
- Check out the Anton Smit National Park, which has some of the most interesting and captivating sculptures anywhere on earth!
- Check out the Emperors Palace Casino and have some fun with your family and friends!
- And, don't forget to visit the Nirox Sculpture Park—where you'd see sculptures made of steel, and could even check out music events, too!

Horseback Africa Website
http://www.horseridinginafrica.com/
Horseback Africa Map
https://goo.gl/maps/cTfJ9PodmuA2
Voortrekker Monument Website
http://www.vtm.org.za/
Voortrekker Monument Map
https://goo.gl/maps/QPCS3Gn2Jck
Walter Sisulu Botanical Garden Website
http://www.sanbi.org/gardens/walter-sisulu
Walter Sisulu Botanical Garden Map
https://goo.gl/maps/MzGnnm4eidK2
Mandela House Website

http://www.mandelahouse.co.za/
Mandela House Map
https://goo.gl/maps/3tpR8kHZWhL2
Honeydew Mazes Website
https://www.facebook.com/Honeydew-Amaizing-Mazes-189457844404099/
Honeydew Mazes Map
https://goo.gl/maps/iFV5ibnWXFp
Anton Smit National Park Website
http://www.antonsmit.co.za/
Anton Smit National Park Map
https://goo.gl/maps/yLr4mis4GY72
Emperors Palace Casino Website
http://www.emperorspalace.com/
Emperors Palace Casino Map
https://goo.gl/maps/D1ZEZdP41AU2
Nirox Sculpture Park Website
http://niroxarts.com/
Nirox Sculpture Park Map
https://goo.gl/maps/Ch8wfbfoqYL2

12

The Best of Limpopo

Limpopo

Meanwhile, there's also Limpopo—the northernmost province of South Africa. This was named after the town's very own Limpopo River that flows on both borders of the province, and is also home to Mapungubwe, a town that houses the most important ancient gold civilizations of South Africa.

Limpopo Map

https://goo.gl/maps/kgCa9Mxft6s
Mapungubwe National Park Website
https://www.sanparks.org/parks/mapungubwe/
Mapungubwe National Park Map
https://goo.gl/maps/UB7UkoxLHCq

Limpopo thrives on tourism as it is one of the three main pillars of their economy. One of the most popular spots here is the world famous Kruger National Park, which as you may know is also part of Mpumalanga Province.

Kruger National Park Website
http://www.krugerpark.co.za/
Kruger National Park Map
https://goo.gl/maps/jUSTe2W2iEM2

Aside from that, there's the Sunland Baobab Farms where an enormous Baobab Tree has been turned into a pub! The tree has been hollowed to make way for a pub and a wine cellar, and the tree is historical in such a way that it is around 1,060 years old already!

The tree has two parts that is connected by a narrow passage, and is known to have survived fires back in the 1800s to 1900s—making it really strong on its own! Fancy a drink there, and you'd have experienced one of the most creative and unique dining experiences of your life!

Sunland Farms Big Baobab Tree Website
http://www.bigbaobab.co.za/
Sunland Farms Big Baobab Tree Map
https://goo.gl/maps/Qia1HXRmZr12

In Limpopo, you could also have the adventure of a lifetime by visiting the Kinyonga Reptile Centre where you could learn more about snakes, Iguanas, and other reptiles in Limpopo. The Baobab is also nearby so you won't have a hard time especially when it's too sunny or hot. This way, you'd learn to appreciate reptiles more! A Pancake restaurant is also nearby.

Kinyonga Reptile Centre Website
http://www.kinyonga.net/
Kinyonga Reptile Centre Map
https://goo.gl/maps/8CSvwuPbHjv

Another beautiful, serene sanctuary is the Debengeni Waterfall which would definitely take your breath away! It has crystal clear waters and a gorgeous setting that would help you to be thankful and more appreciative for nature! It's great to take a walk or sit down by the river here.

Debengeni Waterfall Website
http://www.magoebaskloof.co.za/debengeni-waterfall
Debengeni Waterfall Map
https://goo.gl/maps/vPdLHQ6Tfeu

There's also the Marakele National Park where you could spend time with lions and their cubs—and could even stay in tented camps to really help you feel one with this wildlife sanctuary! Safari tours are also available in the said area.

Marakele National Park Website

https://www.sanparks.org/parks/marakele/

Marakele National Park Map

https://goo.gl/maps/23tUQWJxKru

The Nylsvley Nature Reserve is also around. Here, you can see various birds of every color and could have some peace away from the city. The state of the park is in tip-top shape, too!

The Nylsvley Nature Reserve Website

http://www.nylsvley.co.za/

The Nylsvley Nature Reserve Map

https://goo.gl/maps/2kKL8pccRkq

The hot springs at Mabalingwe Nature Reserve are also worth checking out. It's a different kind of experience that would help you relax and rejuvenate after a long day of walking! A trip to the Echo Caves might also be great if you need more adventure!

Mabalingwe Nature Reserve Website

http://mabalingwe.co.za/

Mabalingwe Nature Reserve Map

https://goo.gl/maps/bikR8SXu1xm

And of course, if you want to lounge around and eat some cheese, you could do so at the Geluksfontein Goat Cheese Farm. According to tourists, the place is not just all about the cheese—their shakes are to-die-for, too!

Geluksfontein Goat Cheese Farm Website
http://geluksfontein.co.za/
Geluksfontein Goat Cheese Farm Map
https://goo.gl/maps/7CyYP7k7H472

Your trip to Limpopo would surely be peppered with excitement and adventure—from wildlife, to cheese, and a tree pub, it will definitely be unforgettable!

Top 10 Things to Do:

- While in Limpopo, don't forget to:
- Visit the Moholoholo Wildlife Rehab Center, where you'd see how wild animals are being taken care of and are allowed to live in their own sanctuary.
- Check out the Hoedspruit Endangered Species Centre, where you can see lions and cheetahs and understand how the people of

Limpopo are working to provide these cheetahs with a brighter future.

- Visit the Bambelela Wildlife Care and Vervet Monkey Rehabilitation Farm. Here, you could learn more about Vervet Monkeys and even get to feed and hug them!
- Visit the Welgevonden Nature Reserve and learn more about this old town in Limpopo—complete with uniquely structured houses you'd never see anywhere else!
- Set your feet in the Mapungubwe National Park, a small but definitely picturesque and unforgettable park!
- Feed yourself at Bitong and Braai Padstal—you can choose your own fresh, organic foods!
- Check out the Mokolo Dam, a hidden reservoir that will help you feel one with nature!
- Take care of baby animals at Mystic Monkeys and Feathers Zoo!
- Have some fun at the Meropa Casino and Entertainment World!
- And, watch the Roots of Rhythm Cultural Experience—a one-of-a-kind experience you won't soon forget!

Moholoholo Wildlife Rehab Center Website
http://www.moholoholo.co.za/
Moholoholo Wildlife Rehab Center Map
https://goo.gl/maps/ZvEgF1x2iwR2
Hoedspruit Endangered Species Centre Website
http://hesc.co.za/
Hoedspruit Endangered Species Centre Map
https://goo.gl/maps/icFzEvscg4K2
Bambelela Wildlife Care Website
http://www.bambelela.org.za/
Bambelela Wildlife Care Map
https://goo.gl/maps/h7XV2EyPLAG2
Vervet Monkey Rehabilitation Website
http://www.vervet.za.org/

Vervet Monkey Map
https://goo.gl/maps/UL9n3kR63bK2
Welgevonden Nature Reserve Website
http://www.welgevondengamereserve.org/
Welgevonden Nature Reserve Map
https://goo.gl/maps/uucWWcWxGat
Mapungubwe National Park Website
https://www.sanparks.org/parks/mapungubwe/
Mapungubwe National Park Map
https://goo.gl/maps/wvJV5Krr9m22
Mystic Monkeys Website
https://www.facebook.com/MysticmonkeysandFeathers
Mystic Monkeys Map
https://goo.gl/maps/82t9Sfc8yEJ2
Meropa Casino and Entertainment World Website
http://www.suninternational.com/meropa/
Meropa Casino and Entertainment World Map
https://goo.gl/maps/8DKVzuxr7JJ2
Roots of Rhythm Cultural Experience Website
http://www.ecoranger.co.za/Roots-of-Rhythm-Culture/
Roots of Rhythm Cultural Experience Map
https://goo.gl/maps/dTVNVUyCdS12

13

The Best of North West

North West

Of course, there's also North West, one of those populous but beautiful places in South Africa. It has parts of both the old Cape and Transvaal Provinces, and is also known as a premier or important province. There are grasslands and scattered trees in the area.

North West Map
https://goo.gl/maps/eoyFFgcAmkM2
North West is quite the Vegas of South Africa. It is home to the Sun City International Casino and Resort, where you could partake

in various games and events, especially during the Beerfest and New Year's Eve! Beach parties(Valley Of The Waves) also abound so you could mingle with your friends and other people, too! There are also lots of bars and restaurants in the area, a casino, and golfing opportunities so you'd always have fun.

Sun City Website
http://www.suninternational.com/sun-city/
Sun City Map
https://goo.gl/maps/6FPWS1Nw7ys
Sun City Golf Website
http://www.sun-city-south-africa.com/golf/

Then, there's also the Lost City Resort, or the Palace of the Lost City that will definitely make you feel like a royal with its grandiose rooms, vast pools, and lush vegetation. It's a good way of being one with nature and forgetting your troubles away! Breakfast is also said to be one of the best, so that's one thing you could look forward to.

The Valley of Waves Water Park is also a great place to see and be in. Basically, you'd have fun just swimming or playing in the pool while seeing these great architecture around you. It'll give you that majestic feeling that no other water theme park could, and you could take loads of pictures, too!

Lost City Resort Website
`http://www.sun-city-south-africa.com/palace-of-the-lost-city
Lost City Resort Map
https://goo.gl/maps/3TifjKEPXNL2
The Valley of Waves Water Park Website
http://www.suninternational.com/sun-city/activities/valley-of-waves/

While in North West, you could visit the Ukutula Lion Park where you could literally walk with the lions and interact with cubs and cheetahs and just feel like these animals are just like us, too! You'd definitely gain love and respect for them after.

Ukutula Lion Park Website

http://www.ukutula.com/

Ukutula Lion Park Map

https://goo.gl/maps/r1zPa5jkTSM2

You might also like the Hartbeespoort Dam. The dam goes in a circle that could really boggle your mind—in a nice way, of course—and you can also eat at the onsite restaurant so you could relax your mind while eating sumptuous food! Finger and fork platters are also available to give you that local, grassroots feel and just help you forget about the hustle and bustle of the city for a while! A Boat Cruise to the area is also available for your convenience. This way, it would be easy for you to appreciate the beauty of the dam!

Hartbeespoort Dam Website

http://www.hartbeespoortonline.co.za/

Hartbeespoort Dam Map

https://goo.gl/maps/mtsgttwYQKC2

You could also try balloon rides and see the province while in the air! It's something that you wouldn't forget for a long time, and might also be a great way to spend time with a special someone! These rides are available at Mankwe Gametrackers Hot Air Balloon Safaris!

Mankwe Gametrackers Hot Air Balloon Safaris Website

http://www.mankwegametrackers.co.za/hot-air-balloon-safaris/

There really are loads of things to do in North West that it would be wrong not to check it out even once in your life! A trip to South Africa would not be complete without it.

Top 10 Things to Do:

- Visit Ukutula Lion Park where you could go on a lion walk, and see those majestic white lions, and even interact with cheetahs and baby cubs!
- Check out Bush Babies Monkey Sanctuary and feel the love of those adorable monkeys!
- Frolic in the waters of Valley of Waves Water Park!
- Be humbled at the Jasmyn Farm Stall where you could see windmills and flowers of every kind! You could eat fresh food here, too!
- Visit the Elephant Sanctuary at Hartbeespoort Dam—one of the most magnificent experiences you could have while in South Africa!
- Have some fun at the Sun City Casino!
- See the crocodiles at Kwena National Farm!
- Go to the Mafikeng Game Reserve and spend some time with giraffes, amongst other animals!
- And, visit the King's Tower(Sun City) and see South Africa from afar!

Bush Babies Monkey Sanctuary Website
http://www.monkeysanctuary.co.za/
Bush Babies Monkey Sanctuary Map

https://goo.gl/maps/ZCqdwtw9Eyj
Jasmyn Farm Stall Website
https://www.facebook.com/pages/Jasmyn-
Hartbeespoort-Dam/373022936127155
Jasmyn Farm Stall Map
https://goo.gl/maps/oCgoQp3RaBn
Elephant Sanctuary at Hartbeespoort Dam Website
http://www.elephantsanctuary.co.za/
Elephant Sanctuary at Hartbeespoort Dam Map
https://goo.gl/maps/8bSSdW6tR5T2
Thaba Kwena Crocodile Farm Website
http://www.tkwena.co.za/
Thaba Kwena Crocodile Farm Map
https://goo.gl/maps/n3VG4ZDRAbv
Mafikeng Game Reserve Map
https://goo.gl/maps/Z8Qtd5RLQ5x

14

The Best of Mpumalanga

Finally, there's Mpumalanga, which literally means the place where the sun rises, and used to be part of the Transvaal Province. Biodiversity abounds in Mpumalanga, seeing as it also is home to the Kruger National Park. The park also offers day tours, safari lodges, and package tours that you can choose from to fit your budget and preferences. Here, you'd see lions, elephants, buffalos, and get to spend time by the river and be around beautiful flowers and plants of every kind!

Mpumalanga Map_
https://goo.gl/maps/xaNfSemKFeu
Kruger National Park Package Tours Website
http://www.krugerpark.co.za/Kruger_Park_Safari_
Packages-travel/kruger-park-classic-lodge-packages.html
Aside from Kruger, you could also visit the Great Limpopo National
Park which has some of the most established wildlife areas in South
Africa. There's also the Sabi Sand Game Reserve which plays host to
various private reserves, such as: Chitwa Chitwa Game Lodge, Idube
Safari Lodge, Savanna Private Game Reserve, Leopard Hills, Inyati,
Exeter, Djuma, and Ulubasa. This way, you won't have a hard time
going from one place to the other and you'd get to enjoy more time
with the animals and with yourself!

Great Limpopo National Park Website
https://www.sanparks.org/conservation/transfrontier/
great_limpopo.php
Great Limpopo National Park Map
https://goo.gl/maps/CPCT3nDkZEp
Sabi Sand Game Reserve Website
http://www.sabi-sands.com/
Sabi Sand Game Reserve Map
https://goo.gl/maps/cpUYnjpuJoD2
Chitwa Chitwa Game Lodge Website
http://www.chitwa.co.za/en/
Chitwa Chitwa Game Lodge Map
https://goo.gl/maps/Zx8kXxUHH7M2
Idube Safari Lodge Website
http://www.idube.com/static
Idube Safari Lodge Map
https://goo.gl/maps/Aj2J6gKHa2y
Savanna Private Game Reserve Website

http://www.savannalodge.com/
Savanna Private Game Reserve Map
https://goo.gl/maps/BzLorWA5q8t
Leopard Hills Website
https://www.facebook.com/LeopardHills
Leopard Hills Map
https://goo.gl/maps/ohugBBKsP6p
Inyati Website
http://www.inyati.co.za/
Inyati Map
https://goo.gl/maps/UrNqwVkouhk
Exeter Website
http://www.andbeyond.com/exeter-river-lodge/
Exeter Map
https://goo.gl/maps/GuBDDzKvEvm
Djuma Website
http://www.djuma.com/
Djuma Map
https://goo.gl/maps/mzCVPNCWDhP2
Ulubasa Website
https://www.facebook.com/Ulusaba/
Ulubasa Map
https://goo.gl/maps/CrHmA8eiNVP2

Then, go and visit the Matsamo Cultural Village. This would take you into an exciting, colorful, and vibrant adventure that would help you learn more about the Matsamo indigenous people of South Africa. You can eat local food, and get to watch a show that they prepared especially for you! It's a good way of understanding where you are—and knowing why it's great to respect these people, and the nature around you. This also goes for Shangha Cultural Village where you could watch cultural dances in the evenings, and make you feel one with the people of Mpumalanga.

Matsamo Cultural Village Tour Website

http://www.crocodilekruger.co.za/activities/matsamo-cultural-village-tours.htm
Matsamo Cultural Village Map
https://goo.gl/maps/mEUqMzMBmjH2

You could also check out Long Tom Cannon(close to Sabie) and Pilgrims Rest, two important facets of the Anglo-Boer War that could help you understand this bygone era without consulting books. It would be unforgettable and inspiring as you'd also get to see the whole province from the mountains!

The Alanglade House Museum is also a favorite of many as it goes to show the early days of Mpumalanga. From there, you could visit Horse Shoe Falls in Marloth Park where you could relax and just be in awe of these breathtaking falls in front of you. The bumpy ride would certainly be worth it!

Long Tom Cannon Website

http://www.sabie.co.za/gallery/cannon.html

Long Tom Cannon Map

https://goo.gl/maps/VS6VgYhuQEu

Pilgrims Rest Website

http://www.pilgrimsrest.org.za/

Pilgrims Rest Map

https://goo.gl/maps/Zs8gmJqJSUk

The Panorama Route is a route that you do have to set foot on. While it may be scary at first, once you reach the end of the road, you'd be in awe of how majestic South Africa looks.

The Panorama Route Tours Website

http://www.africanbudgetsafaris.com/locations/panorama-route/

Then, you could end your trip with a visit to God's Window. Just sit down, bask in the beauty of nature, and breathe fresh air in. It would be a good way to just be thankful for where you are—and who you are.

Your trip to Mpumalanga could conclude your whole South African Journey. There are just so many animals and plants to see, and so many monuments and museums to learn something from. By checking these out, your trip would be so worthwhile—and definitely unforgettable!

Blyde Canyon (God's window) Website
http://www.foreverblydecanyon.co.za/
God's Window Map
https://goo.gl/maps/KpowsYuWuMQ2
Top 10 Things to Do:

- Visit the Kruger National Park and see hyenas, lions, and even wild dogs in their natural sanctuaries!
- Check out the breathtaking Blyde River Canyon that offers some of the most picturesque views in all of South Africa!
- See the amazing birds at Dullstrom Bird of Prey Rehabilitation Centre!
- Relax and reflect at the Bourke's Luck Potholes!(Blyde River)
- Travel back in time with a visit to the historic Sudwala Caves.
- Have some snacks and let your sweet tooth indulge in Shautany Chocolatiers!
- Sample some local food at the Farmers Market!
- Check out the Nicomazi Game Reserve and see some of the most amazing animals on earth!
- Check out God's Widow and be in awe of those fantastic views.
- And, spend some time with people and check out the cultural show at Matsamo Cultural Village!

Dullstrom Bird of Prey Rehabilitation Centre Website

http://www.birdsofprey.co.za/
Dullstrom Bird of Prey Rehabilitation Centre Map
https://goo.gl/maps/jZTD6ib4U2q
Bourke's Luck Potholes Map
https://goo.gl/maps/hwf6xx2dB4z
Sudwala Caves Website
http://www.sudwalacaves.com/
Sudwala Caves Map
https://goo.gl/maps/vGJEXqEsVWv
Shautany Chocolatiers Website
http://www.shautany.co.za/
Shautany Chocolatiers Map
https://goo.gl/maps/DaduY8djZmr
Nicomazi Game Reserve Website
https://www.facebook.com/Nkomazi/
Nicomazi Game Reserve Map
https://goo.gl/maps/KmUmBgpNNYU2

+

15

Conclusion

I want to thank you for reading this book! I sincerely hope that you received value from it . I hope you now have a better idea of what this amazing country has to offer.

This document is geared towards providing exact and reliable information in regards to the topic and issue covered. The publication is sold with the idea that the publisher is not required to render accounting, officially permitted, or otherwise, qualified services. If advice is necessary, legal or professional, a practiced individual in the profession should be ordered.

— From a Declaration of Principles which was accepted and approved equally by a Committee of the American Bar Association and a Committee of Publishers and Associations.

In no way is it legal to reproduce, duplicate, or transmit any part of this document in either electronic means or in printed format. Recording of this publication is strictly prohibited and any storage of this document is not allowed unless with written permission from the publisher. All rights reserved.

The information provided herein is stated to be truthful and consistent, in that any liability, in terms of inattention or otherwise, by any usage or abuse of any policies, processes, or directions contained within is the solitary and utter responsibility of the recipient reader. Under no circumstances will any legal responsibility or blame be held against the publisher for any reparation, damages, or monetary loss due to the information herein, either directly or indirectly.

Respective authors own all copyrights not held by the publisher.

The information herein is offered for informational purposes solely, and is universal as so. The presentation of the information is without contract or any type of guarantee assurance.

The trademarks that are used are without any consent, and the publication of the trademark is without permission or backing by the trademark owner. All trademarks and brands within this book are for clarifying purposes only and are the owned by the owners themselves, not affiliated with this document.

Made in the USA
San Bernardino, CA
27 May 2016